Letters to Us

Izzy Monville

BookLeaf Publishing

Presentation by *BookLeaf Publishing*

Web: www.bookleafpub.com

E-mail: info@bookleafpub.com

ISBN: 9789357440776

First edition 2023

DEDICATION

Too Miss Walsh, who without this would've been impossible.

ACKNOWLEDGEMENT

This book, like every other crazy project and late night idea before it was brought to life with the continued support of my friends and family.

Thank you for reading every bad draft, outline, and title, and listening to every idea that got turned into this book.

Thank you to my family, for supporting every writing project including and that led to this one.

Thank you to my teachers, especially Miss Walsh, who pushed me to become the writer I am today.

Adams Elementary School, September 7th, 2008

Dear Lily,

We learned to haiku
And it made me think of you
Of your fancy words

We learned
Cinquains as well
I don't like them as much
(Don't tell Miss Brown I passed you this)
See you

With love,
Liam

Adams Elementary School, September 7th, 2008

Dear Li,

Haikus are pretty,
About nature, leaves falling.
I thought you'd like them.

Cinquains
Are fun, I love
Their pretty words and their
Humongous possibilities
For all

Love,
Lily

Adams Elementary School, September 7th, 2008

Dear Lily,

I think Miss Brown saw
Our notes. I wonder if she'll
Like our poetry?

If not
At least we had
Our fun. Though how could she
Not? They're brilliant, a true mas-
terpiece.

Love,
Liam

North River Middle School, February 14th, 2012

Dear Lily,

The Dance-
Are you going?
The event of the year
Come party until dawn with me Let's Go!

With love,
Liam

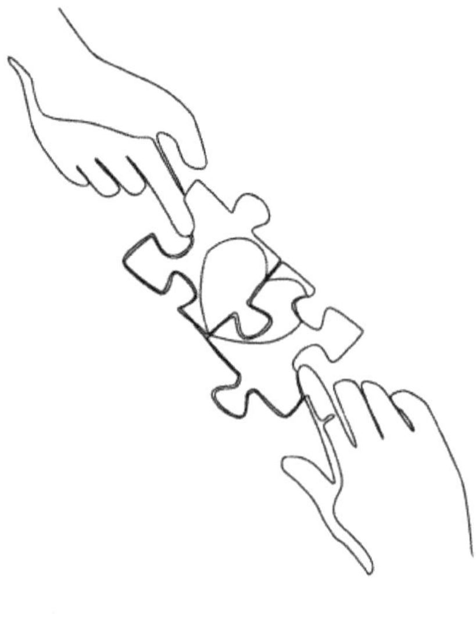

North River Middle School, February 14th, 2012

Dear Li,

Your flowers are so cute

I admire the pursuit

Of course, I'll go with you

I've been waiting on you, it's true Your poetry is quite astute

Love, Lily

Spring Hill High, September 31st, 2014

Dear Liam,

Same people, new place
new structures, new ideas,
into high school, we go.

Still, my mood remains
a melancholy cloud
following my every step.

It stabs me, runs up
from behind to remind me
of your betrayal.

I don't think
I believe you when you say
nothing happened.

The way you looked
when you looked at her
won't leave me.

I think this may be
my last poem until writing
stops stinging.

Love,
Lily

Spring Hill High, October 1st, 2014

Dear Lily,

I must admit
I used to think
Poetry was dumb.
It's short lines
and big omnipotent words,
(I had to google that one).
But for you, I tried.
For you, I'll continue trying.

O
F N
I L
S Y
D Y
R O
WO U'L
F L
O L
CASTLES READTHE
MAKE M FO
L R
L M
I' E

I’ll write syllables
Short and sweet like those haiku’s
The ones you read

Just read them
Read them for me
And know I truly am sorry.

With love,
Liam

Spring Hill High, October 4th, 2014

Dear Lily,

With a heartbreak not long ago
I broke our promises; I know,
Just a teenage calamity.
Ours won't end in fatality.
Please let's not just end this in woe.

We have the time and room to grow,
I promise I'll never let go.
I messed up our normality
With a heartbreak.

No more sorrow to undergo
I know I can't change it, although
To not try is inanity,
Some absolute insanity.
Promise we will not let this go
With a heartbreak.

With love,
Liam

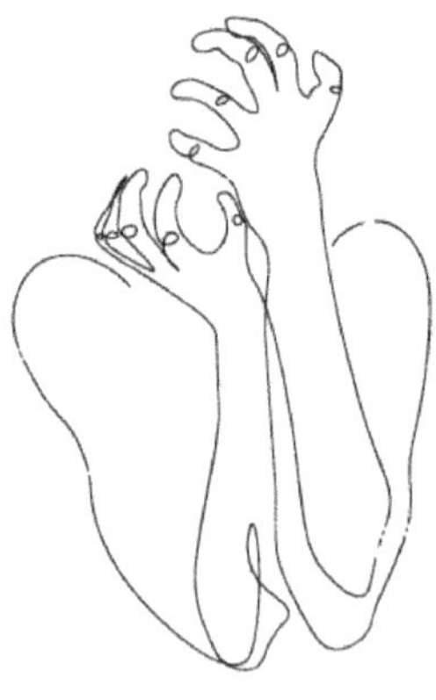

Spring Hill High, October 6th, 2015

Dear Liam,

Your ornate words are misleading
Pretty words won't cut it
Do you think you're succeeding?

Your mistakes are repeating
You might as well quit
Your ornate words are misleading

Are you still completing
Your apology- it's weak, you must admit
Do you think you're succeeding?

Your apology is depleting
Your fault is a funny thing to omit
Your ornate words are misleading

At least your not retreating
Poetry is a waste of your wit
Do you think you're succeeding?

Your confidence is fleeting
You didn't think that'd work, you must admit
Your ornate words are misleading
Do you think you're succeeding?

Love,
Lily

Spring Hill High, May 21st, 2015

Dear Lily,

Because I screwed up,
Regret doesn't cover it.
Of course, I won't waste your time defending myself.
Knowing what I think won't fix this.
Even I know that.
Never stop believing in us, please.

Promises aren't always keepable.
Realities kicked in and I don't like what I see.
Once I would've thought all of this impossible.
Maybe one day I'll wake up and realize this was all a bad dream.
I'm sorry is all I'll say until then.
Sorry is all there is to say.
Except it doesn't fix things, I know.
Sorry about that too.

With love,
Liam

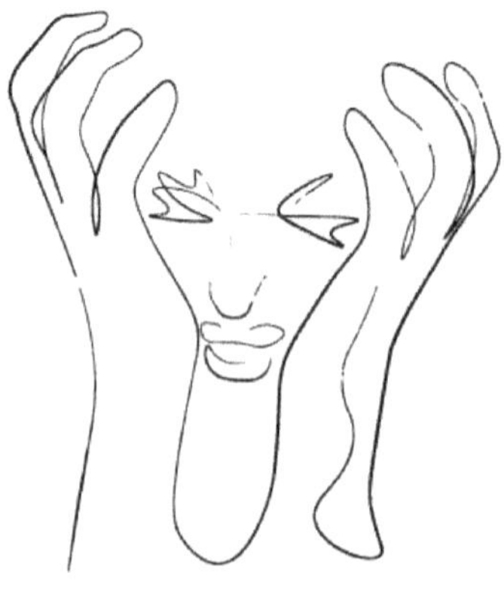

Spring Hill High, May 30th, 2015

Dear Liam,

Neither of us won
In our war of the heart
I think it's over and done
Neither of us won
I haven’t forgotten why we began
But a mark this will impart
Neither of us won
In our war of the heart

Love,
Lily

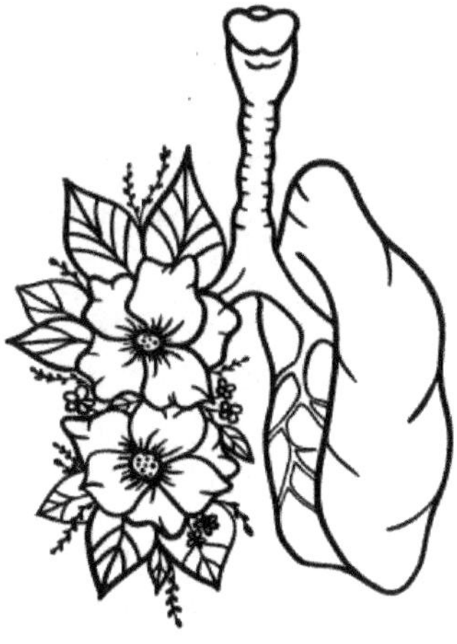

Spring Hill High School, June 20th, 2015

Dear Liam,

I guess I never really said it;
I forgive it all.
It wasn't just your fault, I'll admit

The fault I'll omit.
I don't want this to be our fall
I guess I never really said it.

I'm ready to trust, commit,
I have a feeling we're in it for the long haul.
It wasn't just your fault, I'll admit.

You never quit,
Never stopped, overcame every wall.
I guess I never really said it.

We'll never split,
No matter what darkness befalls
It wasn't just your fault, I'll admit.

My darkest times you lit,
You made my life a ball.

I guess I never really said it;
It wasn't just your fault, I'll admit.

Love,
Lily

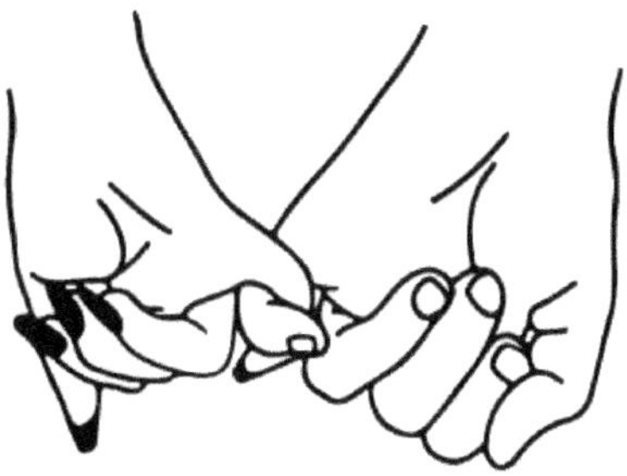

Spring Hill High, April 24th, 2016

Dear Lily,

The dance
In shoes of gold
And suits and dresses alike
Come dance the night away with me
Let's go?

With love,
Liam

Spring Hill High, May 14th, 2016

Dear Liam,

In a long ball gown
dancing the night away
with you beside me.

I felt like I sat on a throne
a crown on my head
as queen of Spring Hill High.

We walked up side by side
as they yelled our names
to retrieve our real crowns.

The bejeweled tiara
watches me from afar
as I betray it to write to you.

The crown meant nothing,
the people, the congratulations less,
but you at my side meant everything.

I suppose
that's what I'm trying to say;
thank you for standing by my side.

Love,
Lily

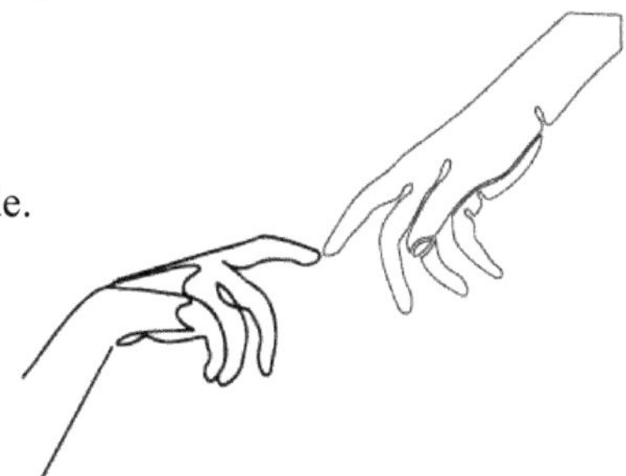

Spring Hill High, May 22nd, 2017

Dear Liam,

In long blue gowns
that took four years to earn
we graduate today.

We'll walk down
for a simple paper
that seems to define us.

The longest walk
with the eyes of our town
judging us one last time.

They love gossip
let's fuel the fire
and never look back.

Small towns confine
let's escape them,
don't look back.

We've got nothing to lose
so run away with me
we won't look back.

Love,
Lily

Spring Hill High, May 20th, 2017

Dear Lily,

We've walked these roads
lived in these houses
for our entire lives.

In the playground where
we first met,
our tree sits.

We'd sit on and
talk for hours
our creaky old porch.

How can we just
walk out on the history
we have here?

Even with the history
this place is my home
because you've been here.

So like a lost puppy
if you go
I'll follow.

With love,
Liam

Spring Hill High, May 20th, 2017

Dear Liam,

Fairview

Minuscule, trivial

Stifling, tiring, dying

Home, family, college, career

Freeing, releasing, liberating

Aglow, alive

New York

Please, just think about it.

Love,
Lily

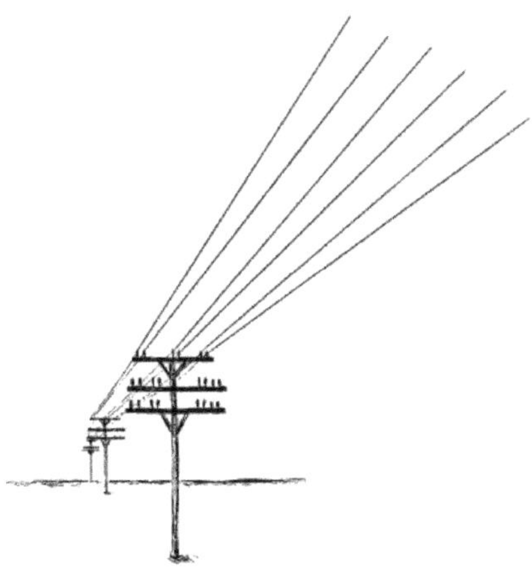

Spring Hill High, May 20th, 2017

Dear Lily,

Alright.
This one marked town
Compared to the whole world?
We'll go explore it together,
Let's start.

Love,
Liam

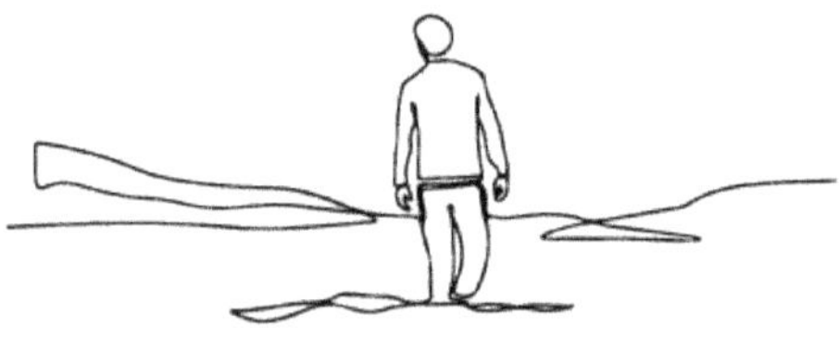

Eiffel Tower, July 13th, 2024

Dear Liam,

You've been so nervous
But I know why
Don't think you're too sly
But I'm at your service
I'll make it easy for your purpose
No need for goodbyes
I know what you were going to imply;
It's forever for us

Marry me?
Down near the sea
Say yes to the rest of our life
Let me be your wife
Promise forever with me
Marry me

With love,
Lily

Rome, Italy, September 28th, 2025

Dear Lily,

They say it's
bad luck seeing the bride
before the wedding.

So I suppose I'll wait
to say you look beautiful
but I'm impatient.

I won't wait
to say I can't wait
for our forever.

For whatever today brings,
for everything we did to get here,
for whatever the future holds.

For getting a dog,
maybe a kid or two,
all together.

For the future,
for a house filled to the brim
for the rest of our lives.

With love,
Liam

Rome, Italy, September 28th, 2025

Dear Liam,

Donned in a white gown
Walking down to you
Your smile the brightest around.

Just an aisle to walk down
Till we're ready to start something new
Donned in a white gown.

I'm here for every birthday countdown
And every breakdown too
Your smile the brightest around

A final ride through town
Seeing how much we grew
Donned in a white gown

Head held high with a crown
A future together in view
Your smile the brightest around

Starting a family of our own
Smiles bright and true
Donned in a white gown
Your smile the brightest around

Love,
Lily

www.ingramcontent.com/pod-product-compliance
Lightning Source LLC
Chambersburg PA
CBHW051758130826
49812CB00033B/1190
* 9 7 8 9 3 5 7 4 4 0 7 7 6 *